IT'S NOT JUST A PHONE CALL

Written by a former insider.

Learn exactly how phone scammers think — and how to stop them cold.

Milton Lomax

IT'S NOT JUST A PHONE CALL

Copyright © 2018 by Milton Lomax

miltonlomaxofficial@gmail.com

Second Edition

ISBN 978-9-7790-5714-9 (Paperback)

ISBN 978-9-7790-5713-2 (eBook)

Printed and bound in the United States of America

First Printing, December 2018

Second Printing, May 2026

> *"If the product is free, then you are the product. If you are not paying for anything, you are not the customer — you are the product being sold."*

> *"Honesty is the first chapter in the book of wisdom."*— Thomas Jefferson

IT'S NOT JUST A PHONE CALL

To everyone who has ever helped me.

To everyone who believed in me — and everyone who didn't.

To my family and my friends.

To Mody, the one who kept pushing me forward.

To Monika, Petya, and Frank.

To the wonderful people I have in my life.

To my readers, my customers —

and to every person I ever cheated, lied to, or set up:

I am giving you this book.

Contents

"Go and get yourself a better job.
A job you will be proud of.
A job you will tell your kids about."

— She said to me.

Introduction

Every day, millions of people receive phone calls they don't understand.

Who is this? How did they get my number? What do they actually want from me? Is this real — or is this a scam?

So many questions, and yet almost no one has given you a straight answer. Until now.

Here is what makes this book different from anything else you've read on the subject: I was on the other side of the phone.

I worked in a call center. I made those calls. I used the scripts, the tactics, the psychological tricks designed to keep you on the line, lower your guard, and take your money. For a long time, I didn't fully understand the damage being done — until one day, a woman I called said something that stopped me cold:

"Go and get yourself a better job. A job you'll be proud of. A job you'll tell your kids about."

She hung up. And she was right.

That conversation changed everything. It's the reason this book exists.

The problem is massive and growing. The United States, Canada, Australia, and the United Kingdom are all being hit with an avalanche of unsolicited calls every single day — telemarketing calls, robocalls, and outright scam calls. And here's something most people don't realize: the majority of these calls are being made from outside those countries, by people operating in ways that are nearly impossible to trace or regulate.

You may think you're protected because you signed up for the Do Not Call Registry. You are not. The calls keep coming regardless of who you are or where you live.

What you don't know is costing you — in money, in time, and sometimes in your life savings.

This book is going to change that.

By the time you finish reading, you will understand exactly how these calls work — from the very first "Hello" to the moment they ask for your credit card number. You will know how callers are trained to build trust, create urgency, and override your instincts. You will learn how to identify whether a call is legitimate, a sales pitch, or a scam — within the first sixty seconds. You will have your own script, your own rebuttals, and a clear list of what to do and what never to do on a call.

You will also learn that in the United States, scammers can be fined up to $40,654 per illegal call — and you'll learn exactly how to use that against them.

The resources on how to sell and how to scam are everywhere. Search Google or YouTube and you'll find thousands of guides teaching people how to manipulate you. But resources on how to protect yourself? Almost nothing. That gap is what this book fills.

Two things to keep in mind as you read:

First — sometimes you have to understand the weapon before you can defend against it. This book will show you how the other side thinks, so you are never caught off guard again.

Second — after you finish this book, if someone asks you what you bring to the table, you tell them: I bring the damn table.

Because when you truly understand what's happening on that call, you don't get played. You take control.

Let's go.

Chapter 1: Who Is This?

Before we go any deeper, I want you to see exactly what we're talking about. Not statistics. Not warnings. Real calls — the kind happening right now, today, while you're reading this. Three different people. Three different approaches. One goal: to take what's yours.

Betty

She was sitting in her armchair, lying back, trying to get some rest. The television was on but she wasn't really watching it. She is 87 years old, and the days move slowly when you're that age — especially when your sons are busy with their own lives and the house is quiet most of the time.

Betty was lonely. And loneliness, as you'll come to understand in this book, is one of the most powerful tools a scammer has.

Her telephone rang.

Trrn... Trrn... Trrn...

She moved slowly toward it, but her heart was beating faster than her feet could carry her. She hoped it was someone she knew. Someone who cared. She had no idea what was coming.

Rep: "Hello, is Betty there?"

Betty: "Yes, who is this?"

Rep: "This is John calling with Medicare Seniors. How are you today?"

Betty: "Good, what about you?"

Rep: "Glad to hear it. The reason for my call today is that we're updating our medical profiles, and I can see here that you haven't yet received your back support brace — the one that's fully covered by your health insurance. Is that correct?"

Betty: "No, I haven't. My doctor didn't mention anything about it."

Rep: "I understand. This is actually a benefit available to you because you're over 65 and enrolled in Medicare. You're entitled to receive this at no cost."

Betty: "I don't really have the kind of pain that would make me need a brace."

Rep: "I hear you. I'm talking about that pain that comes and goes — nothing severe, just that occasional discomfort. I actually have it noted here in your medical records that you've experienced some back pain, which is exactly why this benefit was flagged for you."

Betty: "Well... how much does it cost?"

Rep: "Nothing at all, ma'am. Your insurance has already covered it completely. I just need to confirm a few details we have on file — your name, address, and date of birth."

Betty: "Alright."

And just like that, he had her. Name. Address. Date of birth. Medicare claim number. Secondary insurance information. Everything he needed.

Every time Betty raised a concern, he had an answer ready — smooth, reassuring, and completely rehearsed. She didn't buy anything. She didn't feel pressured. She just thought someone was finally looking out for her.

That's the point. That's how it works.

Robert

He had just come back from a long run. Shower, breakfast, a good morning — he was feeling strong. When his phone rang with an unknown number, he hesitated. But he picked it up. He wasn't worried. He could handle a phone call.

Robert: "Who is this?"

Rep: "Is this Robert Williams?"

Robert: "Speaking. Who are you?"

Rep: "This is Mark calling with Credit Card Services. How's your day going so far?"

Robert: "Never mind my day. What's this call about?"

Rep: "Because you've made your payments on time for the past six consecutive months, you're eligible for a lower interest rate on your credit card."

Robert: "Which credit card? And how did you get my number?"

Rep: "We work with over 286 banks across the US — Bank of America, Capital One, Chase, Citibank, and many others. Our records show you currently carry a balance of around \$3,500 across all accounts. Is that right?"

Robert: "That's... correct."

Rep: "And you're paying around 10% interest?"

Robert: "Yes. But how exactly would you lower my rate?"

Rep: "My job is to qualify you, then I'll transfer you to one of our financial advisors who will calculate your new rate. To get started, which card carries the highest interest — that's the one we'll work on first."

Robert was sharp. He pushed back. He asked the right questions. But the rep was trained for exactly that. Step by step, he collected what he needed — email address, cell phone number, Social Security number, card numbers, expiration dates, and CVV codes.

Robert thought he was in control of the call. He wasn't.

Mrs. Smith

It was a good day. She and her husband were having lunch, laughing about old memories — the kind of afternoon that reminds you why life is worth living. The phone rang and she went to answer it, still smiling. Then she saw the caller ID.

IRS.

Her smile disappeared.

Fraudster: "This is James Brown from the IRS. May I speak with Mrs. Smith?"

Mrs. Smith: "Speaking."

Fraudster: "We're calling to inform you that a legal allegation has been filed against you by the Internal Revenue Service. A law enforcement action is currently in process."

Mrs. Smith: "Excuse me — what are you talking about?"

Fraudster: "You are listed as the primary suspect in a case filed by the IRS. The IRS will be placing a lien on your assets — your home, your vehicle. Your bank accounts will be frozen and seized to recover your outstanding tax debt. Your Social Security number will be blacklisted. You will lose access to all government benefits."

Mrs. Smith: "Oh my God." (She started to cry.)

Fraudster: "Ma'am, the local authorities have an arrest warrant and could be at your door at any moment. However — there is still time to resolve this before that happens."

Mrs. Smith: "How much do I owe?"

Fraudster: "$4,586. That includes your pending taxes, legal fees, and late charges."

Mrs. Smith: "Can I pay by credit card?"

Fraudster: "No. We cannot accept credit cards, debit cards, or any bank transfers. This must be paid in cash through government tax payment vouchers. Your bank cannot know about this — if they find out you have a dispute with the government, they will file a fraud complaint against you and freeze all of your accounts immediately."

Mrs. Smith: "Can I at least speak to my attorney?"

Fraudster: "It's too late for that. I'm trying to stop your arrest right now. Once the payment is submitted, I'll contact your attorney personally. But we need to move fast."

Mrs. Smith put down the phone, got in her car, withdrew the cash, and drove to the store.

She was on her way to hand over $4,586 to a man with a fake name, calling from a foreign country, who would never contact her attorney, would never send a receipt, and would never stop — because the moment the money transferred, she became a confirmed target.

Three phone calls. Three completely different people — an elderly woman seeking comfort, a confident man who thought he was too smart to be fooled, and a happy wife who answered on a perfectly ordinary afternoon.

None of them saw it coming.

And that is exactly why this book exists.

Chapter 2: What Happened Here?

Let's go back to those three calls.

How did they pull it off? How did Betty, Robert, and Mrs. Smith all end up believing they were talking to someone legitimate?

It starts with the name of the company — and it's more calculated than you think.

The rep can't say "I'm calling from Medicare" — because legally, that crosses a line. Quality control standards flag it. So instead, he says "Medicare Seniors" or "Health Care Specialist" or "Senior Health Support." None of those organizations exist. But they sound real enough that your brain fills in the gap. You hear what he wants you to hear, not what he actually said. That's not an accident. That's the technique.

Then there's the name.

The moment a rep opens his mouth, he's already lying — starting with "This is John" or "This is Mark." The reality is that the majority of these calls originate from India, the

Philippines, and Egypt. Every single person working in this industry has an American name alongside their real one. They use it because the moment you hear a foreign name with an accent, doubt sets in and you hang up. So they train. They practice their American names, their American greetings, their American small talk. Some are convincing. Some aren't. But they keep going regardless, because it only takes one yes to make it worth it.

I know this because I was one of them.

Your Information Is Already Out There

Here's something that will make you uncomfortable: before that phone even rang, they already knew your name, your address, your city, your state, your zip code, your date of birth, and in many cases your Medicare claim number or Social Security number.

How? There is an entire industry built around selling your personal information. They're called leads providers, and they operate openly. A leads provider compiles databases of consumer information — sometimes millions of records — and sells them to call centers, telemarketing offices, and scam operations. The price per record depends on quality. Old, overused leads can go for as little as one cent each. Fresh leads — recently updated, complete with date of birth, SSN, and sometimes credit card expiration dates — can go for eight cents or more.

Ten thousand leads is a standard package. One million is not unusual.

And those leads get sold more than once. Your information doesn't belong to one company. It circulates. The same record gets purchased by multiple call centers running multiple campaigns. That's why you might receive five calls in a week about back braces from five different numbers. They all bought the same list.

When you ask to be removed from their calling list, nothing happens. You're still in the database.

The Do Not Call List Is Not What You Think

I still remember the calls where someone would say, "We're on the Do Not Call Registry — why are you calling us?" And honestly? Those were sometimes easier to close than the people who said nothing.

I once sold a husband and wife specifically because they were on the DNC list. My line was simple: "The reason you're receiving this call is because we don't sell anything — we're here to inform you about a benefit that's already been set aside for you." They relaxed immediately.

The truth is this: the Do Not Call Registry was designed for legitimate businesses that choose to comply with it. Scammers don't comply with it. Overseas operations are largely beyond its reach entirely. Registering your number gives you some protection against honest telemarketers. It gives you zero protection against the people this book is actually about.

What They're Actually Selling

Let me be direct: no one calling you from an unknown number cares whether you need the product.

I called people at 5 and 6 in the morning. That's illegal. I knew it was illegal. I did it anyway, because I was chasing a sale. That's the mentality inside those offices. The goal is to close — to get a yes, to get the information, to get paid. Everything else is noise.

Betty was told her back brace was fully covered by insurance. The rep sent her information to three or four different brace providers simultaneously. Betty didn't receive one brace. She received multiple, from multiple companies, all billing her insurance for the same underlying lead.

When you buy something from one of these calls, your profile gets flagged as a confirmed buyer. Now you're what we called an easy meal. Your information gets prioritized, passed around, and used again. They know you'll say yes.

The Miss Cameron Story

I want to tell you about one call I'll never forget.

Her name was Miss Cameron. She had been scammed three times before. Three times. She was terrified of phone calls, refused to confirm any information to anyone, and made it clear from the first second that she didn't trust me.

Within a few minutes, I had everything I needed.

She thanked me at the end of the call. She said I'd made her day.

Here was a woman who had been burned three times, who knew the danger, who started the call with her guard fully raised — and the training I'd received was enough to walk right through it. When she raised a concern, I answered it with her own words. When she hesitated, I slowed down and let her feel in control. When she pulled back, I gave her a reason to stay.

And at the end of the call, she believed she'd made the right choice.

That's not a victory. That's a warning.

The Recording Trick

In some operations — particularly those selling compound creams and medications — calls are structured in two parts. There's an opener who gains your interest and qualifies you, and then a closer who finalizes the sale. But when the call is transferred to the closer, the customer is coached to say that they were the one who initiated the call.

Why? Because that recording becomes their legal protection. If you ever complain — to a bank, to a regulator, to a consumer protection agency — they play the recording. And on that recording, in your own voice, you say you called them. You say you wanted the product. You say it was your idea.

The game was rigged before the call even started.

What We Do Now

I'm not sharing this to make you feel helpless. I'm sharing it because you cannot defend yourself against something you don't understand.

You now know that your information is already in circulation. You know that the DNC list won't protect you. You know that the company name is designed to mislead you, the personal name is fake, and the accent has been practiced. You know that a yes makes you a target for more calls, and that recordings can be used against you. You know that the script was written specifically to handle every concern you might raise.

Now we study the weapons more closely. Because knowing what the weapon is only gets you halfway there. What matters is knowing how to use that knowledge — and that's exactly where we're going next.

Chapter 3: The Weapon

Every sale — every single one — comes down to two things: making you like them, and making you trust them. That's it. That's the whole game.

For an experienced rep, this isn't difficult. These are people who have made thousands of calls, closed hundreds of sales, and lost enough deals to know exactly what went wrong and why. The best of them don't just handle your objections — they prevent them. They've already mapped out every concern you might raise and built their script around it, so by the time you think of a reason to say no, they've already answered it.

This chapter is their catalog. And you're going to read every page of it.

Page One: The Smile

Why do you think salespeople always sound so happy on the phone? It's not because they enjoy their job. It's because a smile is a tool — and it works even when you can't see it.

When someone sounds warm, upbeat, and genuinely pleased to be talking to you, your brain registers it immediately. You relax slightly. Your guard drops slightly. Nobody wants to talk to someone who sounds flat, bored, or miserable. And the moment a caller sounds like any of those things, you hang up.

But there's a second layer to the smile that most people miss: it signals safety. Scammers aren't supposed to sound happy. So when someone calls you sounding relaxed and cheerful, your instinct says — this must be legitimate. That instinct is exactly what they're counting on.

When a rep can make you laugh — that's a completely different level. I've seen it turn skeptical, defensive customers into people who hand over their Social Security number while they're still chuckling.

I remember one call where a woman was laughing so hard she could barely speak. Her husband jumped on the line, told her it was a fraud call, and told her to hang up. She looked at him and said, "Forget about him, he's crazy," and kept talking to me. I got everything I needed.

I also remember a woman in Florida who stopped me mid-call and said, "I don't believe you're American. Where are you calling from?" I was stuck for a second — and then I remembered a line from the film The Devil's Advocate. I used it on her: "Excuse me, ma'am — did I leave my boots under your bed?"

She burst out laughing. And she was mine.

Page Two: Soft Skills

Soft skills are the personal qualities that determine how you interact with other people: empathy, confidence, humor, the ability to listen, warmth. In a legitimate professional setting, these qualities are genuine. In a call center running scam operations, they are performed — precisely and deliberately — because they work.

When a good rep hears you say, "My wife just passed away," their face immediately shifts. Their tone drops. Their voice fills with something that sounds exactly like genuine sorrow. "I'm so sorry to hear that. I'm sure she's at peace." It sounds real. It feels real. Your brain accepts it as real.

Good salespeople listen not to respond, but to appear to understand. They listen for anything they can mirror back to you — a detail, a concern, a phrase you used. They collect it all and use it to build the impression of a genuine human connection.

If I had to define soft skills in this context, I'd say this: it's the art of acting like a decent human being while having no intention of being one.

Page Three: The First Four Seconds

Research shows that people decide within seven seconds whether they want to continue a conversation with a stranger. Jordan Belfort — whose sales training methods are widely studied and widely misused — pushed that window down even further. His method requires a rep to establish three things in the first four seconds: they must come across as sharp, enthusiastic, and an expert in their field.

This is why calls almost always begin with your name. Starting with your name creates the immediate impression that the caller knows you, that you're expected, that this call has a purpose specific to you. It makes you feel like a person of value rather than a random number on a list — which is exactly what you are.

Page Four: Product Knowledge

Don't make the mistake of thinking you can trip them up with a detailed question. Every rep working a specific campaign becomes, very quickly, a specialist in that one product. They know the features, the benefits, the pricing, the common concerns, and the answers to every question you're likely to ask.

If you ask an average rep, "How long should I wear the back brace each day?" he'll say, "Between ten and thirty minutes."

A great rep says: "That really depends on the level of discomfort you're experiencing and what kind of activity you're doing throughout the day."

Same question. Completely different impression. One sounds like a script. The other sounds like a specialist. By the time you realize the difference, the sale is already done.

Page Five: Tonality

You can't see the person on the other end of the phone. But you can picture them — and tonality is how they paint that picture. Think of tonality the way you think of music: it moves up and down to keep your attention, to build emotion, to signal what's coming next.

There are three core types of tonality: the question, the statement, and the command. Skilled reps shift between all three within a single call — sometimes within a single sentence. Their voice rises when they want your attention. It drops when they want you to lean in. It firms up when they want you to follow a direction.

They also match and mirror your tonality. If you speak quickly, they speed up to meet you. If you speak softly, they soften. If you use certain words often, they start using those same words back. This is not coincidence. It is technique.

Tonality doesn't just make you listen. It makes you enjoy the conversation. And the moment a call becomes something you're enjoying, your defenses are gone.

Page Six: Rapport

Rapport is the feeling that the person you're talking to is somehow like you. It doesn't need to be based on anything real. It just needs to feel real.

Jordan Belfort breaks it down into two core messages every good rep sends without stating them directly: the first is "I care about you" — implying this isn't about money or commission. The second is "I'm just like you" — because people trust people who remind them of themselves.

Anthony Robbins frames it this way: you cannot give people what they want until you know what they need, and you cannot know what they need until you've established rapport. He introduced matching and mirroring as a core technique — physically and verbally aligning yourself with the other person so that, on an unconscious level, they begin to feel you are fundamentally similar.

Dr. Milton Erickson, the pioneering hypnotherapist, understood this better than almost anyone. His belief was simple: "Anything is possible in the presence of good rapport." He matched his patients' body language, pace, and emotional tone — and they left feeling understood.

Over the phone, the physical elements fall away. But everything else remains: voice pace, volume, word choice, emotional tone. Somewhere in that exchange, without any formal agreement, a sense of trust begins to form. You don't choose to trust them. You simply find, at some point, that you already do.

Page Seven: Creating the Need

Here's the uncomfortable truth: people are convinced they need a product before they're asked to buy it.

Creating the need is one of the most sophisticated skills in a salesperson's toolkit. They plant a problem. Then they offer the solution. Because the problem sounds specific — because it sounds like they know your situation — the solution sounds tailored to you personally.

"Sir, I see here you're still carrying a balance of around $3,500 and paying over 10% interest."

"Our records show you've been experiencing some back pain from time to time."

I'll give you a real example. I was once in an interview, sitting in a room with four other candidates. The final test was simple: sell me your phone. One by one, the others went through features, price, battery life. When it was my turn, I didn't talk about the phone at all.

I asked: "Do you own a PC?"

"Yes."

"How many hours a day do you use it?"

"Three or four."

"Here," I said, holding up my tablet. "This is your new PC."

I didn't sell the product. I created the need first. And the people calling you have been doing this every day, for years.

Page Eight: Turning the Table

When you try to take control of the call — when you ask a direct question or push back — a skilled caller doesn't get defensive. They redirect. They answer your question and immediately ask one of their own. Suddenly you're no longer leading. You're following again.

"Is this a sales call?"

"Not at all — we're calling because our records show you haven't yet received your back brace, which is fully covered under your Medicare plan. You are still enrolled in Medicare, correct?"

Your question was acknowledged, technically answered, and immediately buried under a new question that requires your response. The conversation has moved on before you noticed.

The rule is simple: the person asking the questions leads the call. Good reps know this, and they will always find a way to get the questions back in their hands.

You now know the full catalog.

The smile that lowers your guard. The soft skills that make you feel heard. The four-second opening that establishes instant credibility. The product knowledge that sounds like expertise. The tonality that shapes how you feel without you realizing it. The rapport that makes a stranger feel like someone who genuinely knows you. The manufactured need that makes the product feel like the logical solution. And the redirect that puts them back in control the moment you try to take it.

This is what walked into your home every time that phone rang.

Now that you know it — we use it. They built the weapon. We just learned how to aim it.

Chapter 4: DNC

Here is a number worth sitting with for a moment: 226 million.

That's how many Americans have registered their phone numbers on the National Do Not Call Registry. Two hundred and twenty-six million people who looked at the volume of unsolicited calls coming into their lives and said — enough. Take my number off the list.

And the calls kept coming anyway.

What the DNC List Actually Does

The registry was designed to limit solicitation calls from legitimate businesses operating within the United States. Companies that follow the law — and many do — check their call lists against the registry and remove registered numbers. For those companies, the system works.

There are also categories of callers that the law explicitly exempts from DNC restrictions: political organizations, registered charities, telephone surveyors, and companies with whom you already have an existing business relationship. They can call you whether you're registered or not.

But here's what the registry was never designed to stop, and never will: overseas operations running scam calls, illegal telemarketing campaigns, and robocall systems that ignore every regulation because they exist entirely outside the reach of US law enforcement.

The Do Not Call list will reduce some robocalls. It will not stop a single call from a boiler room operating out of Cairo, Manila, or New Delhi.

The Numbers Tell the Story

In 2016 alone, the FTC received five million complaints related to unwanted calls — roughly 200,000 complaints every single month — from people who believed they were protected, who had done everything they were supposed to do, and who were still being bombarded.

Since the registry was established in 2004, there have been 18.7 million total complaints filed.

The number of enforcement actions taken in response? 112.

I'm not saying the DNC Registry isn't trying. I believe it is. But the gap between 18.7 million complaints and 112 enforcement actions tells you everything you need to know about the limits of what any regulatory body can do when the people making the calls are sitting in a different country entirely.

Why They Call from Overseas

Once you understand the economics, the overseas model makes complete sense.

If you're running a call center inside the United States, you're subject to FTC oversight, TCPA regulations, state laws, and the Do Not Call Registry. You face real legal exposure. You have to pay American wages.

Run that same operation from India, the Philippines, Egypt, or Pakistan, and almost none of that applies. US regulators have limited jurisdiction over foreign operators. Local authorities in those countries have little interest in pursuing cases on behalf of American consumers.

And the cost structure is almost incomprehensibly different. A representative working in one of these overseas call centers earns, on average, between $114 and $200 per month.

That is not a typo.

For the price of one American employee's weekly paycheck, an overseas operation can run an entire team for a month — making hundreds of calls a day, using auto-dialers capable of placing millions of calls in a 24-hour period. There are no shift restrictions enforced in any meaningful way. I worked in offices where we called people at 4 and 5 in the morning. We knew it was illegal. Nobody stopped us.

The Florida Month

I want to give you one specific example that has stayed with me.

I was working in a campaign in Cairo — one campaign, in one company, in one city. For an entire month, that campaign called only the state of Florida. Every single day. The same state. The same product. The same script. Different numbers, because when people block one, another one appears.

Some of those Florida residents received the same call every day for thirty days. Some received it twice a day. And some of them bought the product — not because they wanted it, but because they were exhausted and believed that buying would make the calls stop.

It didn't. It made them a confirmed customer. And that made their information more valuable, which meant more calls, from more campaigns, selling more products.

Now multiply that one campaign — in one company, in one city — across every country where these operations run. Across every product category. Across every state. That is what is happening to the 226 million people who registered their numbers and expected to be left alone.

One More Thing About the DNC List

Please — stop telling callers that you're on the Do Not Call Registry and asking them to remove your number.

I understand why people do it. It feels like asserting your rights. But when you say "I'm on the DNC list, you need to take me off your list," you are telling a scammer operating from overseas that you are aware of consumer protection regulations. To a trained rep, that is not a warning. That is useful information.

I closed people who said exactly that. More than once.

Where We Go from Here

The DNC Registry is doing what it can within the limits of what it is. It was built for a different era, for a problem that has grown far beyond its original scope.

We are not going to wait for the system to catch up.

What we're going to do is become the thing they least expect: a person on the other end of the phone who knows exactly what's happening, who knows the script better than the rep reading it, and who knows precisely how to make that call cost them more than it was ever worth making.

We don't need the registry. We are going to become it.

Chapter 5: Scams and Scammers

"If it's too good to be true, it probably is."

No country on earth receives more telemarketing calls, sales calls, and scam calls than the United States. And the methods keep expanding — because every time one approach gets flagged, blocked, or reported, another one takes its place.

Before we go further, let's name them. Here are the most common ways people are being scammed by phone today:

- IRS and government impersonation — callers claiming you owe taxes and will be arrested if you don't pay immediately.

- Medicare and insurance fraud — offers for free braces, creams, or medical devices designed to harvest your insurance information.

- Credit card and bank scams — fake representatives claiming to lower your interest rate or flag suspicious activity.

- Tech support scams — callers claiming your computer is sending errors and they need access to fix it.

- Prize and lottery scams — you've won something, but you need to pay a fee to collect it.

- Romance scams — fake relationships built over weeks or months, ending in a request for money.

- Robocall campaigns — automated messages asking you to press a number or call back.

- Fake charity scams — especially active after natural disasters.

- Jury duty scams — someone claiming to be a sheriff's official saying you missed jury duty and will be arrested.

- Employment scams — fake job offers designed to collect your personal information.

- Investment fraud — convincing pitches for opportunities with high returns that don't exist.

- The *72 transfer trick — callers ask you to dial *72 followed by a number, which silently forwards all your incoming calls to their line.

- Phishing emails disguised as official institutions — your bank, the FTC, Apple, Microsoft, or the IRS — complete with logos, letterheads, and links that look completely real.

This is not an exhaustive list. And every single one of these methods is actively in use right now.

The Numbers

The IRS reported that more than 5,000 victims were defrauded of $26.5 million in a single period beginning in late 2013. The Treasury Inspector General for Tax Administration received reports of approximately 736,000 scam contacts in that same window — with nearly 4,550 victims collectively paying over $23 million.

In 2016, the FBI's Internet Crime Complaint Center recorded 14,546 victims of romance and confidence scams who lost nearly $220 million — up from 5,791 victims and $87 million just two years earlier. That is more than a doubling of both victims and losses in 24 months.

According to the US Department of Justice, at least 15,000 people lost more than $300 million in a single coordinated fraud operation that ran from 2013 onward.

And Americans check their phones an estimated 8 billion times a day — roughly 46 times per person. Every one of those checks is an opportunity for a scammer to get through.

How They Get Your Information

For individual scammers, obtaining your basic information requires almost no effort at all. Sites like Whitepages, ThatsThem, and TruePeopleSearch are publicly accessible to anyone. Your name, address, city, state, zip code, email address, age, and sometimes vehicle information are simply there, available to anyone who types in your name.

This is how a caller can open with: "Hi, is this [your full name] at [your address]?" — and sound completely legitimate before they've said another word. They didn't buy your data. They searched for you.

The Tricks You Haven't Heard About

Most people know about gift card scams and wire transfer fraud. But there are a few methods that still catch people off guard:

The *72 trick.

A caller asks you to dial *72 followed by a specific number. This code activates call forwarding on most phone systems. Every incoming call to your number gets silently redirected to their line. You won't know it's happening until you see the charges.

iTunes and gift card payments.

No government agency will ever ask you to pay a debt using iTunes gift cards, Google Play cards, or any other retail gift card. If someone on the phone asks you to go to a grocery store and buy gift cards, and then read them the redemption codes — they are stealing from you.

Voicemail baiting.

Some operations don't call to speak with you — they call to leave a message. "This is an important notice regarding your account. Please call us back immediately." They leave thousands of these messages and wait. The people who call back are self-selected — they're the ones anxious enough to respond.

The fake FTC email.

Your DNC registration does not expire — once you register your number, it stays registered. Any email telling you otherwise is a phishing attempt.

The People Running These Operations

We share this world with people who will spend eight hours a day calling strangers and threatening them, lying to them, and frightening elderly women into tears — for a salary of $114 to $200 a month plus commission.

Most of them are young. Many are students who need money. The commission structure rewards volume: the more you sell, the more you make. There is no ethical friction built into the system.

I was one of them. I know exactly what that room feels like. I'm not telling you this to excuse it. I'm telling you so that you stop imagining these callers as sophisticated masterminds who are impossible to beat. Many of them are twenty-two years old and reading from a script.

The script is the weapon. And you now know the script better than they do.

What the IRS Will Actually Do

The IRS will always contact you by mail first. Always. They do not call to demand immediate payment. They do not threaten arrest over the phone. They do not ask for payment using gift cards, wire transfers, or cryptocurrency.

If you receive such a call, hang up. Then call the IRS directly at their official number: 1-800-829-1040. That's the entire defense against that scam.

The same principle applies to every impersonation call. If someone claims to be calling from your bank, hang up and call the number on the back of your card. If someone claims to be from Social Security, call the official SSA number. If someone claims to be from law enforcement demanding payment, hang up and call your local police non-emergency line.

They are counting on the urgency they've created being stronger than your instinct to verify. Don't let it be.

Before We Move On

Let me end this chapter the way it deserves to end — with the only questions that actually matter when that phone rings.

Should you hesitate before confirming any personal information? Yes.

Should you hesitate before believing a caller represents any institution? Yes.

Should you hesitate to ask for their information — name, company, number, supervisor? No. Ask every time.

Should you feel guilty hanging up? No. Never.

Should you feel obligated to stay on the line because someone is being friendly? No. Friendliness is a technique.

Should you trust anyone who calls you with an offer that sounds too good to be true? No. You already know what that means.

One last thing — a small request, from me to you:

Because the moment you hang up — you win.

Chapter 6: The Script and the Rebuttals

"Better safe than sorry."

Never say yes over the phone to someone you don't know.

You've read their catalog. You know the smile, the soft skills, the tonality, the rapport-building, the manufactured need, and the redirect. You know how the call is structured, where the information goes, and what happens to you after you say yes.

Now it's your turn.

This chapter is your training. By the end of it, you'll have your own script, your own rebuttals, and three specific strategies for handling any unsolicited call — from the quickest exit to the full takedown. You choose which one to use based on the call, your mood, and how much damage you want to do.

The Script

Every call center gives its representatives a script — a written guide covering everything a rep says from the moment you pick up to the moment the call ends. It includes the opening, the reason for the call, the qualification questions, the pitch, and the close. It also includes every likely concern you might raise — and the prepared answer for each one.

A weak rep reads the script. You can hear it — the flat tone, the misplaced pause, the robotic greeting. Most people hang up immediately.

A strong rep has internalized the script so completely that it no longer sounds like a script. It sounds like a conversation. And that's when it works.

The weak rep: "Hello... this is... calling with... how are you today?"

The strong rep: "Hello, may I speak with Mr. —?"

The difference isn't what they say. It's how they say it. You already know this. Now use it.

The Rebuttals

Rebuttals are the responses to your objections — prepared, rehearsed, and used every day. When you say "I'm not interested," there's a rebuttal for that. When you say "I'm on the DNC list," there's a rebuttal for that. When you say "How did you get my number?" — there's a rebuttal for that too.

This is not improvisation. Every concern you raise has been anticipated, written down, practiced, and refined over thousands of calls. The rep doesn't have to think. They just have to listen for the trigger and deliver the response.

The script was built specifically to handle you. Now we're going to build one that handles them.

A Note on Non-Verbal Communication

Research consistently shows that roughly 55% of human communication is body language, 38% is vocal tone and inflection, and only 7% is the actual words being spoken. On a phone call, body language disappears entirely — which means that 93% of your communication comes down to one thing: how you sound.

When you use the samples below, your voice must match your words. Confident delivery. No hesitation. If you sound uncertain, you invite a rebuttal. If you sound clear and settled, the call ends on your terms. It's not what you say — it's how you say it.

Your Three Samples

Here are your three options. Each serves a different purpose and requires a different level of engagement. Read all three. Know all three. Then choose based on the situation.

And before we begin — remember: you always have one more option available. Don't pick up the phone in the first place.

Sample 1: Cut the Long Story Short

Purpose: End the call immediately. Zero engagement. Zero information given.

> **Rep:** "Hello, may I speak with Mr./Mrs. —?"
>
> **You:** (Pick one) "They passed away." / "There's nobody here by that name." / "Wrong number." / "You've reached [a business / a hospital / the police station]."

Then hang up. Immediately. Do not wait for a response.

This works because the moment you make yourself unqualified as a lead, the rep has no path forward. They'll mark you as unqualified — which means your number gets pulled from that campaign's active dial list.

Two things to remember:

- If you say someone has passed away, be prepared for a follow-up directed at the spouse or another household member. Hang up before they get the chance.

- Delivery matters. Say it calmly and with complete confidence. The moment you sound uncertain, you've given them an opening.

You closed the call before they could close you. That's the win.

Sample 2: Play Time

Purpose: Engage on your terms, gather information, give nothing away, and make them work for a sale they'll never get.

This sample is for people who know what they're doing and want to have a little fun doing it. You stay on the line. You act interested. You ask questions. You give no real information.

Rep: "Hello, may I speak with —?"

You: "Speaking. Who's this?"

Rep: "We're calling today because..."

You: "Sounds good. But before we go any further, can I get your name, your company name, and a phone number I can reach you at?"

Rep: "We're calling from a hotline — you can't reach us directly."

You: "I'm not giving you anything until you give me something first. Name, company, phone number."

At this point, one of two things happens: they hang up, or they give you something. Either outcome is a win.

A few lines to keep in your back pocket for Sample 2:

- "Can you send something in the mail?" — Legitimate companies can. Scammers usually can't.

- "What country are you calling from?" — Watch how quickly the tone changes.

- If they insist they're calling from a specific state: "Your number doesn't match that area code."

- If they can't send mail, won't give a number, and can't answer basic questions — you already have your answer.

Sample 3: Game Changer

Purpose: Collect real evidence. Report them. Fine them. Stop them permanently.

This is for the hunters. It requires patience — but the payoff is real.

Here's what most people don't know: anyone who violates the National Do Not Call Registry or places an illegal robocall can be fined up to $40,654 per call. That's a real, enforceable penalty — and private individuals can take action to trigger it.

To use Sample 3, you need three things: a recording, a phone number or company name, and patience.

Start recording the moment you answer. Act interested. The opener — the first person who calls — usually won't give you much. Their job is just to qualify you and transfer the call. The closer, the second representative, is where the useful information lives. They're more likely to provide a company name, a callback number, or enough identifying information to act on.

Do not give them your real information. A wrong address. A wrong card number. Stay on the line, stay interested, and collect everything they give you.

Once you have it:

- File a complaint with the FTC at reportfraud.ftc.gov

- Report the robocall at donotcall.gov

- Contact a consumer protection attorney — many work on contingency for TCPA violations

- Document everything: date, time, what was said, what information they provided

When you report them and enforcement follows, you're not just protecting yourself. You're stopping calls for every person on that lead list.

The Quick-Reference Table

Here's how the three samples play out against a standard call. Keep this somewhere accessible — behind your phone, on your fridge, wherever you'll actually use it.

QUICK-REFERENCE: REP vs. YOUR THREE SAMPLES

Rep: *"May I speak with —?"*
Sample 1: "They passed away." / "Wrong number." [hang up immediately]
Sample 2: "Speaking. Who's this?"
Sample 3: "Speaking. Tell me more." [begin recording]

Rep: *"We're calling because..."*
Sample 1: —
Sample 2: "What do you have for me?"
Sample 3: "Send it over. Enroll me now."

Rep: *"You've been selected / qualified..."*
Sample 1: —
Sample 2: "I must be lucky. Can I get your number?"
Sample 3: "What do I have to do?"

Rep: *"I need to verify your information..."*
Sample 1: —
Sample 2: "You already have it — read it to me."
Sample 3: "Go ahead." [give wrong information]

Rep: *"Can you grab your card?"*
Sample 1: —
Sample 2: "I don't have it handy. Can you send an email?"
Sample 3: "Just a second." [stall, keep recording]

Rep: *"Hold on for a representative..."*
Sample 1: "Wrong number." [wait for live rep, then deliver]
Sample 2: "You called me before — why couldn't I reach you back?"
Sample 3: "Who is this?" [record everything]

Rep: *"We can't give you a callback number."*
Sample 1: —
Sample 2: "Can you send an email? Anything at all?"
Sample 3: "Call me later then." [you're already recording]

What the FTC Says — And Why It Doesn't Fully Protect You

The law requires telemarketers to identify themselves and state that it's a sales call. It restricts calling hours to between 8am and 9pm. It bans pre-recorded robocalls without prior written consent.

These are real laws. They apply to legitimate businesses operating within the United States.

They do not apply — in any practical sense — to a call center operating in Cairo, Manila, or Karachi. I know this, because I was making those calls. We called people at 4, 5, and 6 in the morning. We never identified ourselves as salespeople. We ignored removal requests. And no one came for us — because from where we were sitting, no one could.

The government is working on this problem. But while they work, you need to work too.

It's Your Call

You've reached the end of the training. Now it comes down to a decision — and every single time that phone rings from an unknown number, you'll make it again.

It's your call whether to use Sample 1 and end it in ten seconds, or Sample 2 and make them work for nothing, or Sample 3 and turn the call into evidence.

It's your call whether to give your information to someone you've never met, whose name is fake, whose company doesn't exist, and whose only goal is to take something from you.

I've shown you the whole picture. I've opened the door. Everything from here — it's your call.

Chapter 7: Dos and Don'ts

*"Old ways won't open new doors — and
you can't expect change if you're not
willing to make one."*

This chapter is your reference guide. Everything you've learned in this book lives here in short, usable form — the things you should do when that phone rings, and the things you should never do under any circumstances. Keep it. Come back to it. Share it with someone who needs it.

The Dos

1. Let unknown calls go to voicemail. You always have the option not to answer. If it's important, they'll leave a message. If they don't, that tells you something too.

2. Know your three samples before the phone rings. Sample 1: cut it short. Sample 2: play time. Sample 3: game changer. The best time to decide which to use is before you pick up, not after.

3. Ask for their information before you give yours. Name, company name, and a callback number. Every legitimate caller can provide all three. Most scammers cannot.

4. Verify before you call back. Search the number first. Call the official number of the organization they claim to represent — the one on your card, on their official website, or on your Medicare materials.

5. Talk to someone you trust before making any decision. If a caller is creating urgency and telling you there's no time to consult anyone — that urgency is the scam.

6. Treat your phone number like sensitive personal information. Your cell phone number can unlock accounts, verify identity, and give access to your personal data. Give it only to people you know.

7. Use your mental judgment, not your emotional response. When a call makes you feel excited, afraid, grateful, or rushed — pause. That feeling was engineered.

8. Hang up immediately when you hear: "This call is being recorded for quality assurance." / "I'm going

to recap your information." / "Do we have your permission to..." / "Let me confirm your information once more." These are the sounds of someone building a record they intend to use against you.

9. Hang up immediately when you hear: "Can you hear me?" / "Are you the homeowner?" / "Am I speaking with...?" These are designed to capture a clear "yes" from you on a recording.

10. Ask for everything in writing. If a caller claims you're owed a benefit or that there's a service available to you — ask them to send it by mail or email. A legitimate company can do that.

11. Report everything. Scam calls: reportfraud.ftc.gov. Robocalls: donotcall.gov. IRS impersonation: tigta.gov. If you've shared financial information: contact your bank immediately.

12. Use available call-blocking tools. AT&T and T-Mobile both offer free scam-blocking services. Your smartphone likely has a built-in spam filter — make sure it's turned on.

13. Remember that your information doesn't disappear after a call. The moment you provide information, it is stored, shared, and sold. Assume it will be used again.

14. Know that Medicare changed its claim numbers in April 2018. Numbers are now a combination of letters and digits — no longer the same as your Social Security number. This is still sensitive personal information.

15. Remember: it is never rude to hang up on a scammer.

The Don'ts

16. Don't say "yes" to opening questions you didn't expect. "Can you hear me?" "Are you the homeowner?" Instead of yes, say: "Who is this?" or hang up immediately.

17. Don't confirm your identity. Never confirm that you are the person being asked for — unless you've already verified who is calling and why.

18. Don't give your information to anyone who called you. Not your Social Security number. Not your Medicare claim number. Not your bank account or credit card number — not the full number, not the expiry date, not the CVV.

19. Don't wire money, send gift cards, or use prepaid debit cards to pay anyone who called you. No government agency, bank, or legitimate company will ever ask you to pay through these methods.

20. Don't trust the name or number on your caller ID. Caller ID can be faked. A number that appears to be from your bank, from the IRS, or from a local number may be routing from anywhere in the world.

21. Don't believe that a caller represents the IRS. The IRS contacts people by mail first — always. If someone claims to be from the IRS and demands immediate action, hang up and call 1-800-829-1040.

22. Don't believe that Apple or Microsoft is calling to warn you about your account. Neither will call you unsolicited to report a security issue.

23. Don't believe the FTC is calling to tell you your DNC registration has expired. It hasn't. Registration never expires.

24. Don't click links in unexpected emails or text messages. Scammers send fake emails and texts that appear to come from your bank, Medicare, Apple, or the FTC. Go directly to the official website by typing the address yourself.

25. Don't let them rush you. Urgency is a weapon. Any legitimate caller will give you time to think. The moment someone tells you there's no time to think — take all the time you need.

26. Don't ask to be put on their Do Not Call list. For overseas operations, this accomplishes nothing — and worse, it signals that you're engaged enough to argue.

27. Don't be flattered by: "You've been specially selected." / "Congratulations — you've won a prize." / "This investment carries low risk with higher returns than anything else available." These phrases are scripted. None of them are true.

28. Don't believe that being nice means being trustworthy. Warmth, humor, and charm are techniques — and the best reps use them better than most people you'll meet in real life.

29. Don't buy something to make the calls stop. It won't work. Buying confirms you as an active customer, which guarantees more calls.

30. Don't let loneliness make you vulnerable. If you're home alone and miss having someone to talk to — a cold caller is not the answer. They will use that need against you.

31. Don't let them lead the call. The moment they're asking the questions and you're answering, you've lost the lead. Keep the questions on your side.

One Final Reminder

If a caller claims to represent Medicare, your bank, the IRS, or any organization you have a relationship with — and you have any doubt at all — do this:

Tell them you'll call back. Hang up. Find the official number yourself. Call that number and ask whether they contacted you.

This one habit will protect you from almost every impersonation scam in existence.

You now know what to say, what not to say, when to engage, and when to walk away. All that's left is to use it.

From this point forward — it's your call.

Chapter 8: Why Seniors?

*"Sometimes all we need is someone to pay
attention — someone who will listen,
someone who shows they care, even if
they have to fake it."*— Milton Lomax

There is a reason seniors are the most targeted group in telemarketing and phone scams. It is not because they are foolish. It is not because they are weak. It is because they are lonely — and loneliness, as we've seen throughout this book, is the most powerful weapon a scammer has.

The Reality of Their Days

Many seniors in the United States — those over 65 — live alone or with a spouse who may also be in declining health. Their children have moved away, built their own lives, and visit once or twice a year if they're lucky. Some seniors go weeks without a real conversation with anyone who matters to them. Some spend Christmas alone, or with a pet for company.

Their days are quiet. Their phones don't ring much. And when they do ring — when someone on the other end asks for them by name, speaks warmly, listens patiently, and seems genuinely interested in their well-being — something in them opens up.

They're not being naive. They're being human.

And the people calling them know this. They're trained for it. Soft skills, rapport-building, active listening — all of it is sharpened specifically for this moment. It doesn't take much to close an elderly customer. You just need to show up, be kind, and listen. The sale closes itself.

I know because I did it.

What It Looked Like From My Side

I remember a woman who called back asking to speak to my supervisor — not to complain, but to say kind things about me. I hadn't sold her anything. I had simply listened to her and treated her like a person. When I handed the phone over, I heard her say: "I just want to put some good words in for Milton. He is a wonderful man. He is the best person I've ever spoken to. Promote him. Let him train everyone. He's just in the wrong job."

She wasn't wrong about the last part.

I had another customer who insisted on inviting me to her home. Another who spent thirty minutes telling me the story of how she met her husband — and when she finally finished, one short line closed the sale. She was happy. She felt heard. She trusted me. And when you trust someone, you don't stop to wonder whether they might be lying to you.

That trust is not a flaw. In any other context, it's exactly what we hope people will extend to each other. What makes it painful is that it was exploited — deliberately, systematically, by people who were paid more when they exploited it better.

Enrolled Again and Again

A senior who has bought a product — a back brace, a cream, a medical device — does not simply receive that product and move on. Their information is kept. Their record of saying yes is kept. And they are enrolled again. In the same product, from a different provider. In a related product, from the same campaign. In something else entirely, sold by a company that bought their data.

I worked in offices where a single customer would be enrolled in three or four different brace providers simultaneously. They didn't receive one brace. They received multiple — each one billing their insurance, each one generating a commission, each one adding another layer of information to a profile that continued to be sold.

They often don't understand what's happening. They remember one call. They don't know there were four.

The Things Nobody Talks About

I need to tell you some things that rarely make it into public conversations about phone scams — things I witnessed firsthand.

When a senior expressed frustration or simply wore out a rep's patience, some reps retaliated. They would order food delivery to the customer's address. They would pass the number around to other reps to receive random calls throughout the day. Small, petty cruelties — directed at people who were already isolated and already vulnerable.

Some reps, when they had enough information, would impersonate the customer entirely — calling other companies speaking as that person, as a family member, or as a caregiver — to enroll them in additional products. They had the name, the date of birth, the Medicare number. That was enough.

And the recordings — the records that were supposed to be evidence of what the customer agreed to — were edited. Sections removed. The yes kept, the hesitation cut out. A clean record that showed consent where there had been confusion or pressure.

I'm not telling you this to shock you. I'm telling you because these weren't rare exceptions. I saw them regularly.

Why America Specifically?

I've been asked this question many times: why is the United States the most targeted country for phone scams?

I think you can answer it yourself now.

Americans, in general, are trusting people. Not naive — trusting. There's a difference. When someone is friendly, Americans tend to respond with friendliness. When someone seems to be helping, Americans tend to believe they're being helped. That quality builds marriages, friendships, and communities.

On the other end of a scam call, it costs them their savings.

The woman who told me she'd been called and informed she'd won $100,000 — but needed to pay $8,000 first to claim the prize — paid the $8,000. She got nothing in return. She was embarrassed. She shouldn't have been. She trusted someone who used every technique in this book to make himself believable.

What You Can Do Right Now

If you have a parent, grandparent, aunt, uncle, or elderly neighbor — someone who lives alone, who doesn't get out much, who would genuinely light up when the phone rings — please have this conversation with them.

Not once. Regularly.

Tell them that Medicare will never call them — only mail them. Tell them that no one offering something free over the phone is actually offering something free. Tell them that a person can sound warm, caring, and completely trustworthy while intending to take everything they have.

And if they're not sure what to do when a call comes in, teach them Sample 1. Just two words — "passed away" or "wrong number" — and then hang up. It sounds too simple. But it works.

Take their hand. Walk them through it. You might be the only person in their life who does.

To the Fraudsters

You asked why the United States is the most targeted country for scams.

You know the answer. You've always known it.

What you don't know yet is that it's ending.

Not because the government caught up. But because the people you've been calling — the ones you thought were easy, the ones you counted on to pick up the phone and trust the voice on the other end — they know now.

They know your name isn't John. They know you're not calling from Florida. They know Medicare doesn't make outbound calls. They know what "I'm going to recap your information" means. They know about the three samples.

And they're not alone anymore.

Chapter 9: Alrighty

*"Sometimes a new beginning is even
better than a happy ending."*

We made it.

Before I close this book, I want to say something clearly. I am not against telemarketing. I am not against sales calls. Legitimate telemarketing, conducted within the law, is a real industry. If that's what every call was, this book wouldn't exist.

What I am against — what I will always be against — is this:

Forcing you to buy something you don't need. Lying to you. Misleading you. Calling you at 4, 5, or 6 in the morning. Selling your information without your knowledge. Abusing your kindness. Delivering something completely different from what was promised. Breaking the law. And above all — scamming you.

You are not, to me, a sale. You are a person who picked up this book because something happened — a call that confused you, a charge you didn't authorize, a moment where something felt wrong but you couldn't name it. You deserved to know the truth. Now you do.

The Business Behind the Calls

Most calls you receive fall under lead generation — the process of identifying and cultivating potential customers for a product or service. Within that, there are two primary models:

CPL — Cost Per Lead: the caller is paid when they generate a qualified prospect, regardless of whether that person buys.

CPA — Cost Per Action: the caller is paid only when a specific action is completed — a sale, a sign-up, a form submission.

Here is what those leads are worth per conversion to the businesses running these campaigns:

- Medical Life Alert device: approximately $100

- Solar system installation lead: up to $200

- Loans: approximately $100

- Back braces: $40–$160 depending on insurance type

- Compound creams: starting at $50

- Cancer genetic testing (CGX): up to $300

- Diabetic testing supplies: up to $200

- Cardiac diagnostic tests: up to $300

Now you understand why they call. Now you understand why they call back. Now you understand why, when you buy something once, the calls don't stop — they multiply. Your confirmed purchase makes your lead more valuable. Your information gets sold to campaigns running completely different products. Everyone takes their share.

And you are the one funding all of it.

I worked in offices where they didn't wait for your primary care doctor's approval. They had their own doctors who would sign off on the product without any involvement from the physician who actually knew you. Everyone takes their share of the cake — and you don't have to wonder why, when you know you are the cake itself.

B2B — When They Target Businesses

The calls don't stop at individual consumers. If you run a business, you've likely received calls promising to place you on the first page of Google, improve your search rankings, or grow your customer base.

Many of these operations run from the same overseas locations as the consumer scams. Some maintain physical representatives inside the United States to meet clients in person, backed by American phone numbers that ring back to overseas offices.

The Google ads pitch is a common example. What you may not be told is that the company takes fifty percent of your entire advertising budget before spending anything on your business. And genuine first-page Google placement requires ongoing monthly investment that was never fully explained at the start.

Watch carefully who you trust — and who you give access to your business finances.

The LinkedIn World

When I decided to leave the company I was working for, I started running my own operation from home — and LinkedIn was where that world lived.

In the sales and telemarketing space on LinkedIn, you will find four types of profiles: real clients — legitimate businesses looking for lead generation services; brokers — middlemen who connect call centers with clients; fake profiles — people based in India, Pakistan, Egypt, and the Philippines presenting themselves as US-based businesses; and real call center operators running the rooms, the dialers, and the campaigns.

My profile presented me as a client based in the United States. Once my connections passed 500, real clients began reaching out. Brokers followed. Call center owners offered to send me leads. The whole ecosystem, visible and searchable, operating in plain sight.

And what do those clients know about what's happening under their names? More than you'd expect. I've seen clients who were fully aware that the call centers they worked with were calling people at 4am. Who knew leads were being rerouted — your information sent to multiple providers without your knowledge. Who asked for it specifically, because everyone gets paid again each time it happens.

The technology cost to run this entire operation from home today is under $60 per month: roughly $11 for a VPN, $30 for a VoIP calling service, and $15 for a dialer. Or you can rent a full station — computer, dialer, VPN, and calling data — from an overseas call center for $150 to $200 per month per seat.

Payment comes through PayPal, Western Union, MoneyGram, or direct wire transfer. Clean, fast, and almost impossible to trace.

This is the industry. These are the people. Now you know.

The People Who Will Still Say Yes

After everything in this book, some people will still answer the next call the same way they answered the last one.

Not because they're foolish. But because some people are genuinely kind in a way that makes it difficult to be suspicious. Because some people want to believe the world is more honest than it is. Because some people have been alone for a long time and the voice on the phone is the warmest thing they've heard all day. Because some people have been told their whole lives to be polite, and hanging up on someone feels rude.

I understand all of those reasons. I used every single one of them.

If you recognize yourself in any of those descriptions — please don't be ashamed. Be careful. There's a difference.

If You Want to Trust Anyone Over the Phone

Let me leave you with the clearest thing I know:

If you want to trust anyone who calls you out of nowhere, you have two people to choose from. The first one is dead. The second one is you.

Trust your instincts. Trust your hesitation. Trust the part of you that said something feels wrong about this call — because that part of you has been right more often than you've given it credit for.

You don't need anyone's permission to hang up. You don't need a reason. You don't need to be polite to someone who is trying to take your money.

And when Anthony Robbins was asked by people who said they didn't know how to do something, he gave them one answer: Act like you know how. Start there. The confidence comes after.

What I'm Against — Said One More Time

I want to be precise, because precision matters here.

I was never involved in taking money directly from people. That is the truth, and I'll say it plainly.

But I was involved in making people interested when they weren't. In sending them products they didn't need. In confirming information I had no right to confirm. In enrolling people in services they never fully understood. In training other people to do the same things I did, more effectively. In building a system that made all of the above easier and more profitable.

"He that is without sin among you, let him cast the first stone."

I'm not throwing any stones. I'm handing you a book.

The line between telemarketing and scamming is thinner than most people want to admit. I stood on that line for years. I know exactly what it looks like from both sides. And the reason I wrote this book — the reason that woman's words stopped me cold, the reason I kept coming back to what she said about a job you'd be proud of, a job you'd tell your kids about — is that I finally looked at the line clearly and understood that I had been standing in the wrong place.

So to every person I spoke to — every customer who trusted me, every senior who thought I was genuinely calling to help them, every person who gave me their information because my voice sounded kind:

I'm sorry.

I mean that without reservation, without qualification, and without any expectation that it changes anything. It doesn't undo the calls. It doesn't return the information. It doesn't erase the enrollments. But I mean it — fully, and in writing, in a book with my name on it.

Thank You

To every person who made me laugh during a call — genuinely, unexpectedly.

To the people who invited me into their homes, not knowing I was a stranger calling from thousands of miles away.

To the people who said kind things about me that I didn't deserve — especially the woman who told my supervisor to promote me, to let me train everyone, and said I was just in the wrong job.

She was right.

To Mody, who kept pushing me forward when I didn't think I had anything left to say.

To Monika, Petya, and Frank.

To my family and my friends.

To every reader who picked up this book — my customers, in the truest sense of the word. The ones I owe the most to.

And above all — to the woman whose words on the other end of the phone changed everything. The one who said:

"Go and get yourself a better job. A job you'll be proud of. A job you'll tell your kids about."

She hung up before I could respond.

This book is my response.

Because it's not just a phone call.

— Milton Lomax